BUTTERFLIES

A FOLLETT BEGINNING SCIENCE BOOK

SCIENCE EDITOR:

EDWARD VICTOR, ED. D.
Associate Professor of Science Education,
Northwestern University

Tested in the Evanston Public Schools by
JEANNE S. BROUILLETTE,
Curriculum Coordinator, Elementary Schools

Library of Congress Catalog Card Number: 61-15967

BUTTERFLIES

Jeanne S. Brouillette

Sonora Blue

Colorado Hairstreak

Zebra

Illustrated by BILL BARSS

Follett Publishing Company

Chicago

Behr's Blue

Blue
Swallowtail

An Orange Tip

Butterflies are the most beautiful insects.
They live all over the world. Some butterflies
are very small. Some are very large.

The wings of butterflies are covered with
tiny scales. These scales give butterflies
their beautiful colors.

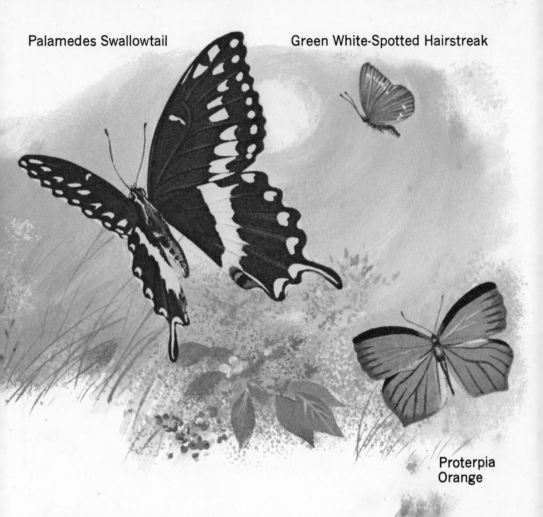

Palamedes Swallowtail

Green White-Spotted Hairstreak

Proterpia Orange

They fly about on warm, sunny days. On cloudy days they do not move about so much. When evening comes, most butterflies hide away in bushes and trees.

5

Head

Thorax

Abdomen

Like all insects, a butterfly has three parts. They are the head, the thorax, and the abdomen.

On the head are two big eyes. These look like round, black beads. Each eye is made up of many, many tiny eyes. With these eyes the butterfly can see in many directions at once.

It has a long tongue, like a thin tube.
The butterfly stretches out this long tongue
to sip nectar from flowers. Nectar is like
perfumed sweet water. When the butterfly is
through feeding, the tongue curls back.

A butterfly has two feelers on its head.
They are called antennae. Each antenna has a
tiny knob at the end. Scientists think that
a butterfly hears and smells with its antennae.

On the middle part, or thorax, are the
wings and legs. Like all insects, the butterfly
has six legs. All butterflies have four wings.

On both the thorax and abdomen, there are
small holes. The butterfly gets air through
these holes.

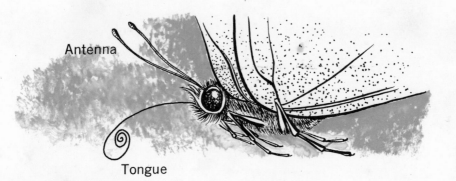

Antenna

Tongue

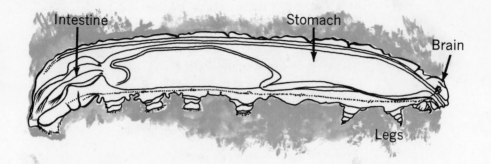

The drawing shows what a caterpillar looks like on the inside.

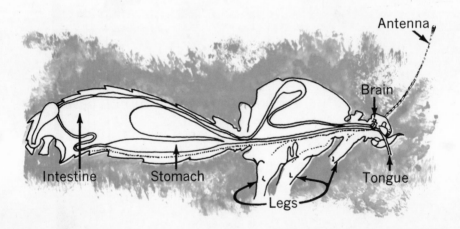

The drawing shows what a full-grown butterfly looks like on the inside.

Eggs

Black Swallowtail
(female)

Every butterfly has four stages, or steps,
to its life. The egg is the first stage.

A mother butterfly lays her eggs on or near
the plant the baby will need for food. A tiny
caterpillar hatches from each egg. The caterpillar
is the second stage. It is called the larva stage.

A caterpillar has six real legs. It has
other parts that look like real legs.

9

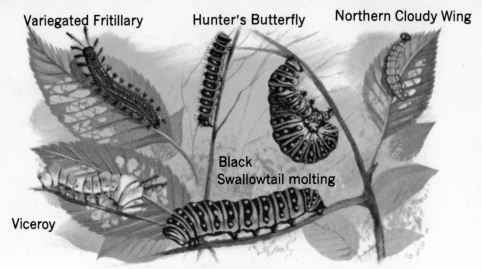

Variegated Fritillary   Hunter's Butterfly   Northern Cloudy Wing

Black
Swallowtail molting

Viceroy

Black Swallowtail

Caterpillars of different kinds of butterflies.

Caterpillars feed on leaves and grow very
fast. Some of them also eat tiny insects.

Soon the caterpillar's skin is too tight.
The skin breaks, and the caterpillar crawls out
of its old skin. Now it has a soft, new skin
that is not too tight.

The caterpillar keeps on eating and eating.
Again the skin gets too tight. It breaks! The
caterpillar crawls out, wearing a new skin.

A caterpillar may shed its skin four or five times. Shedding the skin is called molting.

After the last molting, caterpillars have a resting stage. They attach or fasten themselves to a twig, stem, or fence. The outer skin becomes hard. This is the third stage in the butterfly's life. It is called a chrysalis.

Inside the chrysalis, the caterpillar is now called a pupa. It is changing and growing, but it does not eat.

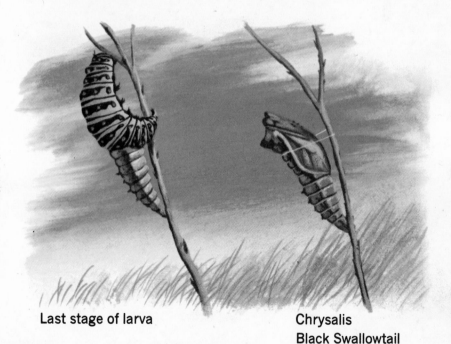

Last stage of larva

Chrysalis
Black Swallowtail

Black Swallowtail

When it is the right time, the chrysalis breaks open. Out crawls a butterfly! This is the fourth stage in a butterfly's life.

The wings of the new butterfly are small and weak. Slowly the butterfly spreads its wings and moves them up and down. Soon the wings are big and strong. Then the insect flies away — a beautiful butterfly.

Chrysalis

Eggs

Mourning Cloak

Caterpillar

Some butterflies live only a few days.
Others live for weeks. And some will even live
through the winter. It is not easy to find them
in winter. They hide away under leaves and rocks,
in hollow trees and old buildings.

The Mourning Cloak hides away in the cold
winter. In early spring this beautiful butterfly
can be seen, sipping nectar from pussy willows.
It lays its eggs in bunches on the twigs of elm
and willow trees.

Chrysalis

Caterpillar

Eggs

Monarch

Some butterflies are named for their colors or stripes. Others get their names from the foods they eat or the way they fly. A few are named for the size or shape of their wings.

The Monarch butterfly is also known as the Milkweed butterfly. It always lays its eggs on the milkweed plant.

Monarchs

This butterfly is a great traveler. It is found all over North America and in South America, too. It is also found in Europe.

When cold weather comes, great flocks of Monarch butterflies fly south. In the spring, each one flies north again. They do not return in flocks. Monarch butterflies live where milkweed plants are found.

Viceroy

Eggs

Caterpillar

The Viceroy butterfly looks very much like the Monarch, but it is smaller. Its caterpillar may sleep all winter, rolled up in a leaf. The Viceroy caterpillar feeds on willow and poplar leaves.

16

Painted Beauty   Painted Lady

The Painted Lady is found all over the
world, wherever thistles grow. It is often
called the Thistle butterfly. It has four
eye-spots on the under side of each hind wing.
It sips nectar from thistle flowers. Its
caterpillar feeds on thistle leaves.

A butterfly that looks like the Painted
Lady is the Painted Beauty. But you can tell
them apart. The Painted Beauty has only two
large spots that look like eyes on the under
side of each hind wing. It lays its eggs on
the leaves of plants called everlastings.

Another butterfly, the Red Admiral, may
hide away during the winter. Or it may pass
the winter as a pupa, in a chrysalis. It is
seen flying about even before leaves are on
the trees.

The Red Admiral is one of the few butterflies
that fly at night. It is found in most parts
of North America.

The eggs are laid on nettle plants. The
black caterpillar has yellow spots and red spines.

Red Admiral

Banded Purple

Buckeye

It is easy to know the Buckeye butterfly. It has big eye-spots on the upper sides of its wings. The eye-spots have circles around them.

The Banded Purple is another easy-to-know butterfly. Each wing has a white band. The caterpillar of the Banded Purple feeds on leaves of willow, birch, and other trees.

Diana Fritillary

The butterflies called Fritillaries get their name from the spots on their wings.

The caterpillars eat at night and hide during the day. Many of the Fritillary caterpillars feed on the leaves of violets.

One of the most beautiful of these insects is the Diana Fritillary. The female is blue-black, and the male is orange and brown.

Regal Fritillary

The Great Spangled Fritillary is the largest of this group of butterflies.

The Regal Fritillary lays its eggs in the fall. The caterpillar lives through the winter and makes a chrysalis in the spring.

Most of the butterflies called Swallowtails have tails on their hind wings. The largest butterfly in North America is the Giant Swallowtail. Its caterpillar is a pest to orange growers, because it eats the leaves of orange trees.

The caterpillar of the Black Swallowtail eats the leaves of parsnips, parsley, carrots, and other plants. These caterpillars are easy to find in vegetable gardens.

Tiger Swallowtail
(Brown female)

Two of the Swallowtails are named after wild animals — Zebra and Tiger. The Zebra Swallowtail butterflies have the longest tails. Most of the Tiger Swallowtails are black and yellow. But in the south, some of the females are brown.

American Copper

Scudder's Blue

Edward's Hairstreak

White-M Hairstreak

Common Blue   Under side of Common Blue

The little Common Blue butterfly is often seen in fields and woods. It belongs to a group of small butterflies known as Blues, Coppers, and Hairstreaks.

The caterpillars of the Common Blue are looked after by ants. The ants fight off enemy insects. The ants like to drink a sweet juice that the caterpillars give off from their bodies.

Cabbage

Orange Sulphur

Pearl Crescent

On sunny summer days, flocks of white, yellow, and bright orange butterflies may be seen along the road. These are the Sulphur butterflies. Flocks of them fly over clover fields and stop to sip water at mud puddles.

The White Cabbage butterfly is a real pest. It lays many tiny eggs on cabbage leaves in the fields. These eggs hatch into tiny green caterpillars that eat much cabbage.

The little Pearl Crescent is seen in great numbers, sipping nectar from purple asters by the roadside.

25

Wanderer

Aphids on Alder

Wanderer caterpillar

The caterpillar of the Wanderer butterfly eats insects.

Caterpillars harm many plants when they eat their leaves.

Some caterpillars help plants. They eat tiny insects that are harmful to the plants.

Butterflies help plants when they go from flower to flower to sip nectar. Tiny yellow grains called pollen are found on flowers. Some of the pollen may cling to the butterfly's body, as it moves. When it goes to the next flower, the pollen may fall off. This helps flowers to make seeds, which will grow into new flowers.

Caterpillars and butterflies have many
enemies. Birds eat many of them. But they do
not eat the Monarch butterfly or its caterpillar.
Scientists think they have a bitter taste. The
Viceroy is safe from birds too, because it looks
so much like the Monarch butterfly.

Field mice, frogs, and squirrels eat butterflies.
Some insects feed on them. People kill them by
spraying the leaves of the plants on which they
live.

Butterflies protect themselves from enemies in different ways. They fly away when an enemy comes near. Some of them hide or do not move. The color of the flower may be so much like the butterfly that the enemy does not see it.

Caterpillars may drop to the ground and hide in the grass. Some caterpillars have a strong smell that keeps enemies away. Others have big eye-spots or horns that frighten birds.

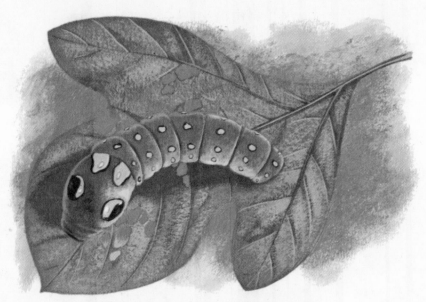

Caterpillar of Green Clouded Swallowtail

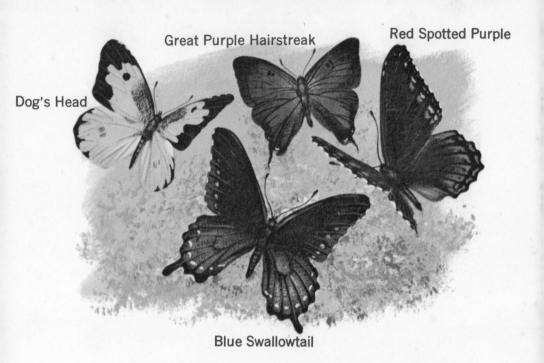

Dog's Head

Great Purple Hairstreak

Red Spotted Purple

Blue Swallowtail

When cold weather comes, some butterflies fly south. Many butterflies die before winter, but a few live through the cold. Butterflies may pass the winter in any of the four stages — as an egg, a caterpillar, a chrysalis, or a butterfly.

They rest and wait for spring. When warm, sunny days come, beautiful butterflies will be seen in gardens, fields, and woods again.

Words Younger Children May Need Help With

(Numbers refer to page on which the word first appears)

3 Colorado Hairstreak
  Sonora
4 Swallowtail
  Behr's
  scale(s)
5 Palamedes
  Proterpia
6 thorax
  abdomen
  direction(s)
7 tongue
  nectar
  antenna, antennae
  knob
  scientist(s)

8 intestine
  caterpillar
9 larva, larvae
10 Variegated Fritillary
  Viceroy
11 chrysalis
  pupa, pupae
13 Mourning Cloak
14 Monarch
15 Europe
17 thistle(s)
  everlasting(s)
18 Admiral
  nettle
  spines

19 Buckeye
20 Diana
21 Spangled
  Regal
22 parsnip(s)
  parsley
  carrot(s)
24 Scudder's
25 Sulphur
  Cabbage
  Pearl Crescent
26 Wanderer
  pollen
27 enemy, enemies

THINGS TO DO IN THE CLASSROOM OR AT HOME

Examine a caterpillar. What colors and markings does it have? What is its shape? Is it larger toward the head or toward the rear end? How many legs does it seem to have? Can you tell which are the real legs? The real legs have little sharp claws and look very different from the false legs.

Touch the caterpillar's head with a small twig or a blade of grass. What does it do? Does the caterpillar give off an odor when you touch it?

Watch the caterpillar as it feeds. Does it eat the whole leaf or does it leave some of the leaf behind?

Keep a caterpillar alive. A large glass jar with holes punched in the lid is a good caterpillar cage. Keep the caterpillar supplied with fresh leaves of the sort it was eating when you found it. If you are lucky you will see the caterpillar shed its skin. How does it act when it is shedding its skin? How does it get ready for this? What does it do?

Collect a chrysalis. If your caterpillar is going to turn into a butterfly, it will turn into a chrysalis first. Look for a butterfly chrysalis outdoors. A chrysalis is easiest to find in the early fall. You will find one stuck to a twig, stem, or fence. It will be almost the same color as the twig, stem, or fence.

Put the chrysalis into an aquarium or a large glass jar. Put a screen or a bit of cheesecloth over the top so the chrysalis will have plenty of air. The aquarium or glass jar should have some earth on the bottom. Add some water to the earth to keep it wet. Do not add much water.

In a few months a butterfly will come out of the chrysalis. Give the butterfly a twig to rest on. Soon the butterfly will spread its wings and let them dry. Dip a piece of cotton into water that has sugar in it and put the cotton near the butterfly. The butterfly may unroll its tongue for you and feed on the sugar water.

Hunt and collect butterflies. If you want to collect butterflies, you will need a butterfly net. Use a stick for the handle, a clothes hanger for the hoop, and any light cloth or net for the bag. A long thin forked stick can be stick and hoop both. You can catch butterflies in your hands or in a jar, but you are likely to break their wings. A net is better.

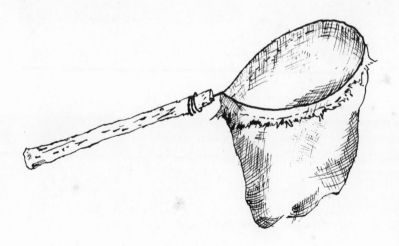

You will need some glass jars to hold the butterflies you catch. Half pint and pint jars with screw caps are good for holding butterflies.

Put some cleaning fluid in the bottom of each jar. Cover the cleaning fluid with absorbent cotton, and pack the cotton down tightly. The cleaning fluid will give off a gas. This gas will kill the butterflies quickly when you put them in the jar. Be careful not to breathe the gas yourself. If the cotton gets dry, pour more cleaning fluid into the jar.

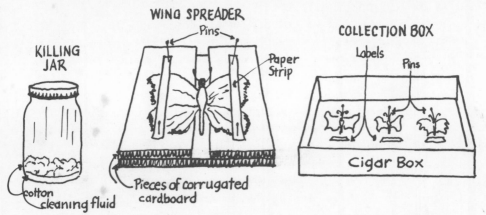

KILLING JAR

cotton
cleaning fluid

WING SPREADER
Pins
Paper Strip
Pieces of corrugated cardboard

COLLECTION BOX
Labels
Pins
Cigar Box

When you catch a butterfly in your net, quickly twist the top of the net so that the butterfly will not get away. Then carefully hold the butterfly and put it into one of your jars. Dry the dead butterfly with its wings spread flat.

Cigar boxes are good to keep the butterflies you catch. First cover the bottom of the box with a layer or two of corrugated cardboard. Spread the butterfly out carefully and put a pin through the middle of it. The butterfly will look prettier with the wings spread out so that everybody can see the beautiful colors.

Pin a small label below each butterfly. On the label print the name of the butterfly, if you know it, the place where you caught it, the date when you caught it, and your name.